80/20 @ School

A Student's Guide to Unlocking the Power of the 80/20 Principle

Lee Davidson

Author: Lee Davidson
Graphics & Cover Design: Robin Crossman
Editing: Erin Korniyenko

Printed in the United States of America

First Printing, 2011

ISBN-13: 978-0-9876772-1-1
ISBN-10: 0987677217

eBook version: ISBN-13: 978-0-9876772-2-8

Canuck Corp.
756 Kelly Drive
Kamloops, BC
V2B 4G4
Canada

DEDICATION

To the 20 percent of people in my life that give me 80 percent of the joy, love and motivation. Thank you!

CONTENTS

ACKNOWLEDGMENTS

Angelina and Liam, thank you for providing me with an understanding of what the truly important things in life are. Lin, thank you for encouraging and believing in me.

Chapter 1

80/20 - WHAT IS IT?

The 80/20 principle is nothing new, in fact it dates all the way back to Italy in the early 1900s. Vilfredo Pareto observed that 80 percent of land and wealth in Italy was owned by only 20 percent of the population. He went on to find other interesting applications for what is known as the Pareto Principle. In more modern times, the principle is simply called the 80/20 principle, and that is how we shall address it throughout this book.

Simply put the 80/20 principle demonstrates that in many aspects of our lives, 80 percent of the output comes from just 20 percent of the input. While the exact ratio is not really that important, what is important is that the closer you evaluate something the more often this rough principle tends to emerge.

The principle can be found in most aspects of our everyday lives, from the use of our time, revenue generated from business or effort expended on customer service. The 80/20 principle is everywhere, and when we understand it we can begin to use it in our favor.

When we really start to link the principle to our everyday lives, we can be quite humbled to learn that the ratio is often even more slanted than what we thought. A simple example could be your Facebook account: what is the ratio of Facebook "friends" you have listed on your account compared to how many of those people you actually talk to or keep in touch with? A safe bet for most people would be the ratio is higher than 80/20, maybe closer to 95/5. Check your telephone contacts or your email contacts and you will probably find the same thing. How about the clothes in your wardrobe? Most people probably wear the same 30 to 40 percent of their clothes over and over while the rest sits on the hanger waiting for an important interview or a special date night.

As I mentioned, the ratio is not the most important part. What is important is being able to identify the principle in the world around us, so that we can use it to our advantage. For the mathematics students out there, it is understood that 80/20 is not the correct format to present the numbers (I have seen it presented 80:20, 64:4, 16:1 and other versions), but I will present and discuss the 80/20 principle, or variations of it, as if we were looking at a pie chart.

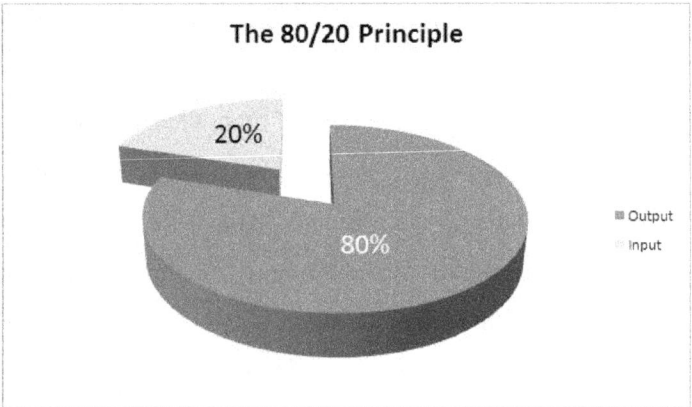

It is important to understand that when you identify the 20 percent inputs that are leading to the 80 percent output, you make strides in figuring out what it is making that 20 percent have such an impact. The 80/20 principle swings both ways; it can show you something positive like how a small portion of your customers make up a large portion of your revenue, or conversely it can demonstrate how a single activity can consume a major portion of your time.

The trick is to identify the 20 percent and figure out how to either focus more on those few customers who generate the largest portion of the revenue pie, or how to better manage your time so that one activity isn't using up all your time resources.

As an example let's look at telephone customer service. In this day and age, when you call an office you will almost always be connected to an automated answering service before you actually get to speak to somebody. While this can be frustrating and annoying when you just want to ask a simple question or book an appointment, there is a very simple and practical reason behind it.

Imagine you are the secretary at a busy office. Your tasks include answering calls and doing other various tasks, while this is extremely oversimplified it will work for this example. In a given day you field 200 telephone calls and 150 are asking you to connect the caller to various office personnel. Let's say each call takes one minute. That is two and a half hours of your day forwarding calls—leaving you four and a half hours to perform your other responsibilities.

Your manager notices that you are not able to complete your other tasks and inquires as to why. You tell him that you spend a large portion of your day doing one task –

forwarding calls. Of course for us the solution is simple; either the firm should hire a second secretary who can field calls while you do the administrative work or invest in an automated call service.

The firm decides to set up the automated call service. Now when somebody calls your office they are first screened by the automated machine asking them to enter the extension they wish to reach. You now have to field only 50 calls a day and you have time to focus on the other administrative duties. As a bonus, you notice you are more cheerful to callers now that you don't use up a large portion of your day saying, "hold please while I connect you".

It is a simplified example, but you can see how by identifying a single task that took up a disproportionate amount of the workday, the firm was able to adjust their way of handling calls and become more efficient.

WHY SHOULD YOU CARE?

The purpose of this book is to take the 80/20 principle and demonstrate a few ways to make you a more effective student. Being a student is demanding on your time, energy, social life and personal economy, so finding a few simple ways to utilize the 80/20 principle during your student years can really help you be a successful student.

Being a successful student does not mean you have to lock yourself away in your dorm room and study all day, sacrificing everything in the pursuit of perfect grades. While being a student does entail sacrifices, with some careful planning and proper motivation you can achieve academic success while still enjoying the many other aspects of college life. The goal is to achieve some sort of balance or harmony with what you need to do and what you want to do. Every student is different in their objectives, but every student can benefit from applying the 80/20 principle at school.

The 80/20 principle is around us every day in just about everything we do. In one way or another we can use the concept behind the general principle to help us become more efficient. This may mean having more free time to spend with friends and family or having fewer conversations with the person who gives you the most headaches. Whatever your priorities are, understanding the 80/20 principle will open your eyes to how many opportunities in your normal routine you have to apply it to.

In the following chapters I will discuss themes like time management, motivation, study techniques for success, speed reading techniques and other issues that will equip you with a few ways you can become a more efficient student. Along the way I will discuss how to apply the 80/20 principle to various aspects of student life. By the end of the book you will be able to identify ways in which you can become more efficient in your day-to-day life and help yourself achieve your goals.

For the students who find it difficult to juggle study, social life, athletics and personal time, this book will help you identify the 20 percent that you need to strengthen or change to help you find a good balance. Other students may actually enjoy spending large portions of their time on one aspect of college life and not feel the need for other types of stimuli. No problem! This book offers you a way to get even more of what you like. That is the entire point of the 80/20 principle. Identify the 20 percent that makes the 80 percent impact and you can begin to manipulate the other variables to get even more output!

A point worth keeping in mind as you work your way through this book is that the aim of this book is not to cover every topic in great depth. As you will learn, the 80/20 principle also applies to this book. I have tried to bring the 20 percent of information that will yield the figurative 80 percent value. At the end of the book you will find further reading suggestions which will help you expand your knowledge and help you dig deeper into some of the themes I cover. It would be counterproductive of me to give hundreds of examples or engage in a long-winded history lesson on the political and economic landscape of Pareto's Italy. So instead I have tried to keep it brief, while still informative.

Chapter 2

TIME MANAGEMENT

An important concept to understand regarding time management is that time goes on uninterrupted regardless of what we do. There are only 24 hours or 1440 minutes in each day no matter what we do, we cannot change that. We cannot "save" time. There is no bank where we can put all the hours we save and withdraw them later to enjoy. Even if we use less time by taking the subway to work rather than sitting in traffic, we can't add up all the "saved" minutes and apply them to our summer holidays. Time marches on no matter if we are on the subway or in a traffic jam. So it is important that we learn to manage our time effectively.

Time management is basically how we use our 1440 minutes each day in the most efficient way possible. Although time can't be saved, it can definitely be wasted. How we use and manage our time is dependent on our needs, wants and priorities.

If you are to be effective in your time management, you must be able to get organized. Being able to identify your priorities and organize them will enable you to use the tools at your disposal to begin to manage your time. There is no shortage of books, blogs, websites and applications out there to help to get yourself organized. However, it is worth taking some caution so as not to get so caught up in organizing your day that you actually end up using a disproportionate amount of time getting organized.

When we begin to set our priorities we can also identify what I refer to as Time Bandits. Time Bandits are the things that do not add anything useful to our daily plan. Time Bandits will be different for everyone. Perhaps checking your Facebook account takes up 45 minutes of your day. If this is something that is rewarding for you, and you enjoy keeping in touch with your friends then so be it. Add it to your list of priorities and you can ensure to carve out some time for this activity. Another person may see Facebook as a complete waste of time, so for this person they could eliminate this Time Bandit from their daily routine.

Whatever your Time Bandits are, the point is to prioritize your activities and eliminate or reduce the ones that don't enhance your overall goal of efficient time management.

For the student, time management is vital to academic success and perhaps should even be taught as a course as it would instill valuable skills which would not only benefit students in school, but in the professional arena after graduation. Students are required to balance course workloads with any number of other activities like part time jobs and social events. To be an effective student requires that you have some tools to be able to start to sort your busy calendar. Otherwise you begin to drown in due dates and other obligations.

FIVE TOOLS FOR TIME MANAGEMENT

Here are five tools that can help a student start to get control over their use of time. I will demonstrate how these tools are useful to you as a student and your day to day time commitments. While wanting to scuba dive with sharks in South Africa may be something you wish to add to your to-do list, it probably won't help you to be a better student this semester. Therefore, I am taking a more short-term, day-in-the-life-of a student approach to how the following tools can help you to better manage your time as a student.

Making a To-Do List: Simple right? Write down the things you need to do, cross them off when you're done. Essentially, yes, this is correct. However, without a little structure a to-do list can turn into a never ending list that ends up looking like a hopeless lost cause, rather than an effective tool of time management. A good to-do list is specific. When you look at the entry you should know exactly what you are supposed to be doing. If I have a term paper due next week, then writing "start term paper" on my Monday to-do list is a bit vague. A better entry would be "write abstract and introduction for term paper". Ok, now I know what I am supposed to be doing and also I know when I have completed this task.

Another important aspect of a good to-do list is to prioritize the items on the list. Use color codes, letters or numbers to signify importance. It doesn't matter what your system is, as long as you can identify what is most important and what can wait.

Prioritize Your List: having your tasks laid out on your to-do list is the first step, but without some way of knowing what is most important, you won't know where to start. Using the Eisenhower Matrix is a simple way to quickly assign your tasks a priority. I use a number system: "1" is for tasks that are urgent and important; "2" for tasks that are urgent, but not important (can I find an alternative solution to deal with this like delegation?); "3" for tasks that are important but can wait; and "4" for those tasks that are neither urgent nor important which I can get to later. Below is a simple example of the Eisenhower Matrix.

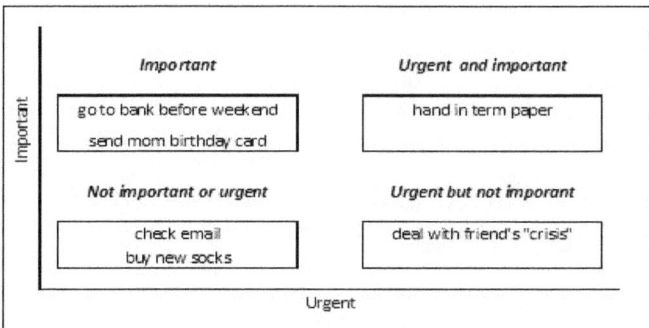

Important		Urgent and important
go to bank before weekend send mom birthday card		hand in term paper
Not important or urgent		**Urgent but not imporant**
check email buy new socks		deal with friend's "crisis"

Urgent

I don't suggest writing the matrix out each time you make a new to-do list, a simpler method is to instead just go down your list and ask yourself which category each task falls into. Assign the relevant number and then get cracking on the list. Again, we don't want to get to the point of diminishing returns here, we just want to be able to quickly sort out our priorities, assign them a spot on the to-do list and get started.

Learn to Schedule: Making a good schedule is important as it will allow you the time you need to do the most important tasks on your list. It will also show you where you have time to fit in other aspects of your life.

The key to a good schedule is to be realistic. If you know you won't study for five straight hours, then there is no point in using a block of your schedule for this unrealistic task. Instead, identify the tasks you want and need to do. Figure out how much time you will need to be effective for each task and assign a block of your daily schedule to it. Do your best to follow your schedule as you will feel a sense of accomplishment when you are able to cross tasks off your list.

Alternatively, do not become a slave to your schedule. A good schedule is flexible enough to be able to adapt to unforeseen events or things not going exactly to plan. Failing to adhere to a strict schedule can make you feel like you are falling behind or unable to accomplish your tasks. So make your schedule realistic and something you can see yourself actually accomplishing.

When planning your schedule, ask yourself when is the best time to accomplish each task. If you want to go to the gym, write two chapters of your term paper and have lunch with friends, how could you fit all this in? Do you work well in the morning? If so, perhaps try to complete one chapter of your paper before meeting your friends and then work on the second chapter after a nice lunch. Do you hate going to the gym when it's full of people? Try to schedule this at off-peak hours. Whatever works best for you is key. Some things like class lectures are scheduled for you, but you still have a lot of flexibility for where you can fit your other priority tasks into your day.

Manage Distractions: Now that you have done the work to create an organized to-do list and an effective schedule, you are ready to get down to work. Time management skills are only as good as your ability to manage distractions. There are countless distractions that will try to knock you off your carefully planned course.

The trick is to manage their impact. If you have a mobile phone that constantly receives text messages, but you really need to study for a solid, uninterrupted hour, then turn your mobile off or to silent. Ask yourself and an honest question: in the last week or month, how many text messages have I received that if I didn't answer within one hour would have resulted in some sort of major catastrophe? Chances are none, so the phone can wait until you have a break. There, you have just managed a distraction.

Distractions will try to creep into your day at every possible chance, each one seeming to be more urgent and dire than the last. Do your best to stay focused and not allow yourself to be taken off course. This may mean finding a better study area, turning down invitations to social events or simple turning off the television. Whatever you can identify as a distraction, you should do your best to avoid it during your scheduled time to work on a given task.

Just Say No: It is ok to say no. Trust me. The first time you feel a bit guilty, but after a while you start to understand there are reasons you have a prioritized list of things to do. If you constantly say yes to every request made of you, you will end up never having time to get to the things that are important.

I am not suggesting you turn into a selfish hermit who never helps out, but it is ok to say no when you actually have something you would rather be doing or need to be doing. The problem with saying yes is that it quickly snowballs, one leads to another and another and suddenly people begin to expect you will always be able to be counted on to pitch in. When you can, go for it. But if the only reason you find yourself saying yes is because you feel guilty, then don't do it. You are allowing yourself to be manipulated and, in the end, it is you who will have to catch up on things that were bumped off your schedule. Remember it is ok to say no.

COMMON MISTAKES

Good time management can be a strong ally during your school and professional careers, but it is also easy to slip away from even the best laid out schedule. Listed below are a few common mistake people tend to make that can undo any time management plan. If you are able to identify and avoid these pitfalls, you will be in a better position to continue to make strong progress with your time management plan.

Taking on Too Many Tasks: Taking on too many different roles, tasks, requests or activities can quickly become overwhelming. Try to limit yourself first to the tasks you must do and try to manage your time so that you also have time to do the extra things you want to do. These will be different for everyone. One person may argue that getting in a swim each morning is a priority for them. If this is true for you, work it into a schedule that you can stay on top of.

Too Few Breaks: It is unreasonable to cram your schedule so tightly that you have only back to back tasks. You need to take enough breaks throughout the day to ensure you actually have the energy to do the things you need and want to do. If you have planned a three hour study session, break it up with a couple of 10 minute breaks for a quick walk, a snack or whatever you need to recharge. You will find you are more effective over the long run when you are not overextending yourself.

Procrastination: We all do it; we all put things off for another day. When you make your schedule remember to make it realistic. If you find yourself constantly putting something off, reevaluate if it is really as important as you think, or if you may need to break the task down into more manageable chunks. The best thing to do is to get started on it and normally once the wheels start turning you will find it easier to keep the engine running.

Multitasking: Being able to multitask may look good on your resume, but in reality it often leads to two jobs being done at less than the desired level. If you can avoid it, work on one project with full focus and then move onto the next. It is better to take a little extra time and have two good projects than to work quickly and have two subpar ones.

HOW THE 80/20 PRINCIPLE APPLIES TO TIME MANAGEMENT

The 80/20 principle applies to the concept of time management by helping us to identify our Time Bandits. What is it that we are spending our time on? How can we become more efficient? What can we change to allow us to do more of the things we enjoy? Once we have unmasked our Time Bandits we can figure out ways to reduce or eliminate them.

If we know that we can't avoid putting in 20 hours a week of study time, then we can at least make sure we are doing it in a way that is most effective. If we really love taking piano lessons after class, but we realize that it is taking up a disproportionate amount of time, then we can make changes in our schedule to either accommodate for it or we may have to realize that it is a Time Bandit.

There are things we simply must do if we want to be successful students. It is assumed that since you have enrolled in University you are interested in actually working towards a degree. So this means that your needs need to come before your wants (most of the time). Using the 80/20 principle will help you figure out how many from both categories you can reasonably take on.

It is important to manage your time for what is actually important. In some of the following chapters you will learn how to apply the 80/20 principle to your school work so that you have time to do more of the things you actually want to do. The topic of the next chapter, Speed Reading, will help you to cut down the mountain of reading you have, while still comprehending the material. If 80 percent of your study time is taken up by reading, then these tips will help you reduce that time so you have more time to work on other coursework or something from your "want to do" list. Remember the value of the 80/20 principle is in helping us realize where we can best put our efforts to produce the most good. If you are using too much effort and getting too little reward, changes need to be made. If you find a small effort is producing a lot of output, you should want to learn how to capitalize on it.

Chapter 3

SPEED READING

Learning how to read effectively is one of the most important skills you can acquire as a student. This chapter is called speed reading, but speed is not the real topic. The reason I have used the term "speed reading" is that I strongly encourage you to find a speed reading workbook or enroll in a course which are most often referred to as speed reading courses/books. Speed reading comes with practice, but comprehension comes from good reading skills regardless of the speed at which you read. There is no value in being able to breeze through 500 words a minute if you have to go back and read it three times to understand it properly.

The aim of this chapter is not to try to teach you to speed read, as that would be an entire book in itself. The aim is to show you some of the tips that will help you manage your reading requirements as a student. It is also worth noting that I will discuss these tips from a students' point of view, referring to the texts as if we were discussing textbooks. Some speed reading techniques are different for fiction, journals, textbooks, online articles and other non-fiction works. By the end of this chapter you should have some tools that will help you to become a more effective reader and hopefully be encouraged to purchase a speed reading book to teach yourself the techniques of this valuable skill.

Speed reading techniques can benefit everyone. You are not being measured against anyone but yourself, and therefore your starting speed is not important. When you learn to read effectively, the speed score will take care of itself. As you learn to use tools like eye focus, previewing and text marking, you will begin to be able to find the 20 percent of the information that will help you most in a much more efficient way. This will help you quickly cut through your reading pile and be able to use less time reading and more time applying the knowledge.

SPEED READING TOOLS

There are many tools at your disposal for speed reading. These include learning to be more efficient with your eye span, the use of different types of pacers, identifying keywords or thought clusters and previewing techniques. Learning to speed read is not a passive activity. You will need to learn about the tools, how to use them and then practice them with a variety of exercises. This depth is beyond the scope of this book, so instead we will focus our attention on a small part of the larger speed reading course (maybe 20 percent, for example!) that I believe will help you to become a more efficient reader. I cannot urge you strongly enough to get a book on speed reading and work through the exercises. It is easily one of the most time efficient things you can do as a student. In addition there are numerous sources available online to help you learn speed reading techniques. One of my favorites is found at *www.acereader.com/education/*. This site offers a free trial and many excellent exercises.

HOW TO READ EFFECTIVELY

In a given school year, a normal student is enrolled in eight to ten classes, each with a text book with an average of six hundred pages. In addition to the textbook, you will be required to read articles, do research, produce your own papers and possibly even read a novel or two for fun. That's a lot of reading and will take up a substantial amount of the time you dedicate to your studies in your time management schedule. So how can you get through these five thousand or more pages of material in an economical fashion? By understanding that the 80/20 principle applies to your reading workload, just like anything else, that's how.

As mentioned earlier, the speed at which you read is not as important as actually understanding what you are reading. The speed will come with practice and combined with the following three tips, your comprehension and retention of the information will become much stronger. Like anything else, the more you practice it and use these tools, the better and more efficient you will become. In no time at all you will be easily cutting your reading pile down and may even have time to start reading for enjoyment.

Background Knowledge: The power of association is a key element in the study of learning. Psychologists, educators and marketers all use association to try to figure out how we learn and retain knowledge. Background knowledge on a subject helps us to form associations with the new information we are learning. When we can create associations between the old and new information, we are making a bond between them. Basically, we are giving our brain a stronger incentive to continue to retain this knowledge.

It is easy for us to get into a subject that we are really interested in, but other course material may seem extremely bland and boring. We need to learn this material in order to be successful on our exam, so apart from just learning it for the sake of learning it, we can give our brains a reason to retain this knowledge long term, rather than just until the exam is over. As a quick example, I struggled with statistics. I understood it and I understood why it was part of our curriculum, but I didn't really begin to appreciate it until I started to see a direct application for it. When I started investing in Forex (foreign exchange trading), the association bridge was easy to build. I could find practical uses for probability and distribution curves. Once I started making money, I appreciated what I had learnt in statistics!

Taking the time to educate yourself on things outside of the course material is never a waste of time. You would be surprised at how quickly your brain begins to make associations with new and old information. When this happens, you are strengthening the need for your brain to store this information.

Knowing What You Are Supposed To Know: Most textbooks are arranged in a similar format to make it easier for students to learn and retain the information. Chapters start with an introduction or overview and may even list learning outcomes or objectives. Before you start to read a chapter it is useful to review the learning outcomes to have a better idea of what you are supposed to be learning about in a particular chapter. Previewing the chapter may seem like it adds time to the overall exercise of reading the chapter, but in reality is doesn't because it allows you to be able to focus on the information that you actually need.

Before reading a chapter I usually browse the learning objectives and introduction. I then flip to the end of the chapter and skim the summary. Most textbooks will also have some questions or discussion points at the end of each chapter. Now I am armed with the knowledge of what I am expected to know by the time I finish the chapter.

By using speed reading techniques like previewing and skimming, I am able to quickly go through each section of the chapter. Because I now know what I am looking for, I can quickly skim the beginning parts of paragraphs to see if I actually need to read the entire section. Often I do not. Additionally authors usually help us by adding notes in the margins and highlighting important key words, terms or phrases. All this makes it much easier to find the information that will allow us to be confident in meeting the learning objectives of the chapter.

In the beginning you may feel a bit uncertain about skipping over portions of the text, but with a little practice you will become better and better at being able to focus on the important material. Learning to preview and skim effectively takes practice and working through a speed reading book will help you learn exactly the techniques you need to master this. At the end of this book there is a section for further reading where you will find notes for a great book on speed reading which is full of these types of exercises.

Text Marking: The highlighter; every student's best friend, right? Maybe, maybe not. If your highlighting pen has dried up by the third week of your course, then definitely not! Highlighting text is a very useful way to be able to quickly find good information which you have already read when you are doing review and study. However, if you have highlighted sentence after sentence, it becomes counterproductive and may be easier to read what isn't highlighted.

When marking text, you should focus on the key words. When you are reviewing your notes at a later date you should be immediately able to recognize why you highlighted this word (or phrase) in the first place. If you have to spend a minute re-reading a paragraph to understand why you highlighted it, then it was not really effective. The reason for marking text is to give your brain a small jolt when it sees the highlighted words.

When highlighting a text, think of yourself as an editor and highlight the application of the paragraph. Often authors will give their hypothesis and then defend it with a real world example. I usually am able to understand more from these examples and this is what I chose to focus on.

Another tip to try is to use pencils or thin highlighters. The thick highlighter can begin to distract you (especially if you use a color system) from the rest of the text, some of which may be useful. Also, as a related word of caution when purchasing used textbooks, if you see that the previous owner has highlighted large portions of the text, you may not want to buy it. It can be distracting to read and also limit what you should be finding on your own in order to actually learn and retain the material yourself.

Since much more of our day to day reading is done online, it is worth taking a moment to address this topic. It may not be practical or necessary to print out everything we need from the internet. For example, a research article we are expected to review for a course. We can still use our previewing and skimming techniques to efficiently work through the article. Some programs may allow us to highlight and save the document, but be careful not to spend a large amount of time doing this. One alternative is to make a mind-map or cluster diagram with pen and paper as you read the online article. It's an alternative to highlighting which is also effective in capturing the important parts you will need to review. We will review taking notes in the next chapter.

HOW THE 80/20 PRINCIPLE APPLIES TO SPEED READING

Using the 80/20 principle when you are working through a textbook chapter is important as few textbooks are meant to be read cover to cover. In many courses the instructor will tell you which chapters are part of the curriculum. Reading a textbook is a bit like searching for gold in a river bed; you have to sift through a lot of other stuff to get to the nuggets.

Focusing on the 20 percent of important material will help us to quickly identify the portions of the chapter we need to prospect in. This is not to say that only 20 percent of a chapter is useful, but when we combine our speed reading techniques with our time management techniques, we begin to quickly find the information we need in order to reduce the amount of time needed to dedicate to working through our reading pile.

Text marking is a great example of the 80/20 principle. We find a few bits of the information that are vital to the learning objectives and focus on these. We then use these as jumping off points to get a full understanding of the important material. Associations with previous knowledge also help to strengthen our learning.

Combining the 80/20 principle and techniques like speed reading are also important when we are doing research. Going through library databases in search of research articles or supporting documentation can be extremely time-consuming. When we are able to preview and skim effectively we can quickly go through articles and identify relevant information that we can dig deeper into if it suits our needs.

The usefulness of the 80/20 principle when reading is to balance the workload we have with the time in which we have to do it. By learning how to get the vital information first we can maximize the output of our allotted time for reading.

CHAPTER 4

HOW TO STUDY

Without knowing how to study effectively you can find yourself on the wrong end of the 80/20 scale very quickly. Implementing good study habits is crucial to all students and is something you need to get on top of early in your academic career. The ability to have good time management skills is only the first step to creating an efficient study system. In order for your study habits to be successful, you not only need to know how to schedule proper time for study, but you also need to know how to make that time truly gives you the most output possible.

Study habits can be tricky because what works well for one person may be a total time-drain for someone else. In this chapter we will examine some typical study tips and how we can boost their effectiveness—or eliminate them from our toolbox—by bringing the 80/20 principle to life in our study system.

A ROADMAP

As previously mentioned, time management skills are important in how you will tailor your study system to best suit you. Once you understand what type of system works best for you, you will know how much time you need to devote from your schedule to getting maximum output for your study time input.

An important step for students is to get a general idea of what is expected of them from a particular class. It would not make sense to go on a long trip without a map, nor does it make sense to start a class with no idea of where you are supposed to end up. Your roadmap starts with two things. The first is your course overview or syllabus which you will usually receive from your instructor at the beginning of the semester. It will detail important information like the topics of lectures, reading passages, assignments and other task-critical information. Take a few minutes and make sure you understand what is expected of you during the course and for the exam.

The second part of your roadmap is your textbook. Getting a general idea of how your textbook is laid out is a good idea. Most textbooks follow a fairly standard format which makes it easier for you to find relevant information, summarize main points, utilize glossaries and reflect on learning objectives as you progress from chapter to chapter.

Just like you would do with a reading article, you should preview the textbook. This gives you an idea of the layout and the material covered. It is also useful to have a peek at the glossary and index to see how much information you can get from there. Most textbooks have a large index that helps to quickly locate key concepts.

Getting acquainted with your textbook will help you to understand how the author has presented his information. Is your textbook heavy on case examples? Are the introductions long and rambling? Does the book use models to help illustrate points? All of this information will help you identify the critical parts of the reading assignments.

Most textbooks follow a similar format. In each chapter you will find an introduction and often there will be learning outcomes or objectives listed. This is important information as it will help you when you deploy your speed reading tactics. Bold faced headings usually help us to identify where one topic ends and a new one starts. As we reflect on the learning outcomes, we can figure out if this is a relevant section or something we can skim. Most authors highlight key terms and concepts throughout the text, indicating that they are important to the theme of the section. This doesn't mean that you need to learn every word in bold print, but it does help you to figure out what the author may think is important. In addition, authors often put helpful notes in the margins.

Some textbooks may have examples which you can review to make sure you understand the concepts. Textbooks for subjects like mathematics, statistics and accounting will probably have many examples that you can follow along with. Most books will also have questions or discussions at the end of the chapter so you can test yourself and see if you grasp the chapter's content.

All of these parts of the textbook are fairly standard over the different subjects, but by making sure you understand the layout of your book you will be in a much better position to use your study tools and speed reading tools in an efficient way. As an extra tip, if your school provides access to previous exams, then you should definitely take the opportunity to review them and find out what kind of information is expected of you, the types of questions you can expect (although don't expect them to be the same) and how examiners expect answers and essays to be written.

STUDY GROUPS

The 80/20 principle can be used to describe study groups both positively and negatively, so the real trick with study groups is to find good group members and to have a plan. Without both of these, study groups quickly fall into the negative category. Study groups can be extremely efficient and effective if organized correctly. As an example, imagine a reading group which assigns one chapter per person who then shares their findings with the group. This reading group exhibits a great way to use the 80/20 principle (each member reads one chapter and takes notes, but get the benefit as if they had spent the time to read and take notes for five chapters). On the flip side, a study group with even one lazy member can completely negate the efforts of the majority.

When you have the option of choosing your study group, do so carefully. You want to make sure it falls within your 80/20 guidelines so that you are actually getting more output than you could by doing it on your own or in less time. You need to weigh the cost/benefit of your group and decide if it a good use of your time to be involved. Below is an example of cost/benefit of a typical study group.

Cost/Benifit for study groups

Pros (+)	Cons (-)
Share ideas	Difficult to schedule
New insights	No control over other's input
Lower workload	Conflicts
Social	Dependency on others

Of course there could be many other variables that you could add to either side of the above table. What is important for you is to identify which side the majority of variables in your group fall on, and then decide if this is a worthwhile use of your limited time resources.

Here are a few simple tips to make your study group more efficient:

1. Be prepared with your portion of the assignment to share in your group.

2. Ensure that everyone is able to contribute to discussions without the fear of being put down for their opinions. You can learn a lot by actually listening to others.

3. Get rid of deadweight. If a group member is not adding value to the group, get rid of them.

4. Stay focused on the reason for the group. If laptops or tablets are not needed, turn them off while in the study group

5. Be realistic with your scheduling. Effective groups need breaks and time to discuss and share thoughts, so schedule accordingly.

6. Be on time.

7. Have a plan and structure before meeting. It is a waste of time to spend the first 20 minutes of study group figuring out what is to be done.

8. Make sure everyone understands the goals of the group. If you have deadlines, ensure everyone knows when to do what.

9. If your group shares notes, email or photocopy your portion to the other group members before the meeting time so everyone has all materials needed during the session.

STUDY ENHANCERS

Study enhancers are tools to help you actually get down to the nuts and bolts of studying. A good study enhancer will give your brain a little jolt and help it to remember the main point. Good study enhancers are brief, but contain the necessary cues to get your mind running and bring forth the information that you have previously stored.

Taking good notes as you read or listen to lectures is important. It is not effective to just sit and copy everything the lecturer says, you need to be able to internalize it into a way that is meaningful to you. Quality notes remind you of the overall theme so you can fill in the blanks on your own. When you can do this from your notes, you are actually learning and imprinting the subject in your brain so you can recall it later. There is a difference between knowing something, and really understanding it. Too often students are satisfied to just know a term and be able to cite the glossary definition, but this won't help you during exams when you need to elaborate and analyze the subject deeper.

Flash cards can be effective if you are able to keep the points brief. Having a flash card with a question or term on one side and the answer on the other is a good way to "flash" memorize important concepts. Be sure to keep the information brief. The idea here is to give your brain a reminder so that you can bring forth the knowledge on your own. Simply rewriting an entire paragraph is no better than just re-reading the book itself.

Mind maps or clusters are another effective tool when studying. Making a drawing as you read with branches to central themes can help you to recall the information when you review for your exams. As with cue cards, the goal is to be brief, a quick note with a branch to other connected topics will help you relate the main concepts with the overall theme of the section or chapter.

Some students find it useful to record a lecture and listen to it afterwards. If this is helpful to you then do so, but you should also combine it with a note taking technique like mind mapping to get the most value. Some lecturers also post podcasts of their lectures online; this can also be a good source of information if you find recording lectures useful. Just be sure to weigh the cost/benefit of going through an entire lecture over again compared to taking good notes during class.

When you can combine techniques you retain more information; you are not only listening, but actively learning by writing or discussing (with a study group) the topic. Some people learn best by sitting in lectures, others fall asleep. Whatever is best for you is how you should shape your study habits.

When you have made good notes from your selected reading or lectures it is important to review them. If you write your notes and then don't pick them up again until a few days before your exam, you will have missed a valuable opportunity to imprint the information on your brain. The diagram below shows how quickly information is forgotten without review.

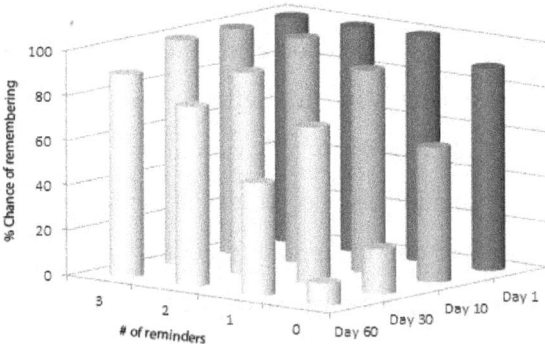

You can see that a person who learns something (day 1) retains about 90 percent of the information. If they do not review the material at all, chances are that by day 60 they will have retained only about 10 percent of what they were taught on day 1. A person who regularly reviews their notes is much more capable of retaining the information long term, and the relationship gets stronger and stronger with each review session. A person who reviews what they learnt 1 day 10 days, 30 days and 60 days after learning it is likely to have retained as much as 95 percent of the information—more than they retained in lecture on day 1! When preparing for exams, this will allow you to have a much fuller grasp of the overall concept.

Trying to cram all the information in at the end of the term will not be as effective as regularly reviewing your material throughout the semester. You can use the 80/20 principle to figure out what information you actually need to review. If you know that one topic is more important than another, you can divert more time to reviewing your notes for that theme.

HOW 80/20 APPLIES TO STUDY HABITS

The 80/20 principle applies to your study habits in two main ways. Firstly, in how you determine what are effective study enhancers and habits for you. What works for one person may not work for another. So it is in your best interest to figure out what gives you the most output for the resources (time, effort, motivation, etc.) you have to give. When you know what works best for you, you can focus on doing more of that type of activity, and less of the ones that don't work.

Secondly, your time is a valuable resource. By using the 80/20 principle, you can divert your time to the study activities that are effective for you. If you find yourself in a work/study group with people who spend too much time socializing or who are unprepared for meetings, then you should do a cost/benefit analysis and decided if your time wasn't better spent elsewhere or with another group.

By eliminating study habits that don't work for you, you give yourself the chance to focus on what does work. I can't use cue cards at all. I have horrible penmanship so I spend too much time trying to make my cards legible. I end up using twice as much time as I would had I made simple mind maps for myself. This is how I focus my energy when I study: I preview a section of text, map out a few main points, skim the rest of the text, map out a bit more, then, if I feel like I have a grasp of the learning objective, I move on. When I go back to review my notes, I can quickly identify the main points and refresh my memory.

Chapter 5

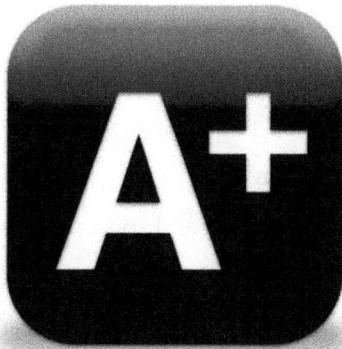

SUBMITTING A GOOD PAPER

In high school you may have gotten away with using flashy fonts, colorful binders and fluffy opinionated content. University is a different game. Essentially there are two important parts to writing a good term paper, the content and the format of the paper. The following tips are also useful for written answers on sit down exams, but for simplicity I will focus on submitting term papers. When you grasp the concept, you will be able to use this for either purpose.

This chapter is outlined a little differently than the others because when you start at university most schools offer some kind of matriculation package or course to help you get acquainted with the schools policies. These generally include how to format papers and plagiarism guidelines. In the interest of following the 80/20 principle, I will not go through the type of information that you will be getting in these types of courses anyway. In addition, you can easily find information online about the structure of articles, research papers and submitted assignments.

Instead, we will just jump right into how the 80/20 principle applies to creating a good term paper. Most schools will have a standardized format they accept for their written assignments. Generally, all subjects in the school will follow this format, but it is worth double checking to be sure. The format covers items like margins, spacing, font, article structure and how to cite sources. Following the proper formatting rules probably won't improve your grade in a course, but failing to follow the rules can definitely hurt your grade.

Generally, you will be required to have certain margins and text spacing to allow examiners to provide feedback, and they will require you to use one of the standardized bibliographic formats like MLA, APA or Chicago style. Papers follow a fairly standard format as well. A submitted assignment may follow a format like:

1. Abstract
2. Introduction
3. Body
4. Summary/Conclusion
5. Bibliography
6. Appendix

Research papers are slightly different and may follow a format like:

1. Title
2. Abstract
3. Introduction
4. Method
5. Results
6. Discussion
7. Bibliography
8. Appendix

Why does this matter when we are discussing the 80/20 principle? You can waste a lot of time trying to format your paper properly if you don't know how, and your effort may be diminished by handing in a poorly formatted paper. So in order to get the most output while using the least input, we will discuss a few ways to cut corners and maximize our output.

At the school library or on the school library website, you will be able to find examples of how the school accepts papers. They may even have a template you can download. If so, download and save it as it will have all the margins, pager number requirements, header/footers and table of contents already set for you. Once you have this template you don't need to recreate it over and over for each submitted assignment over the next few years. Additionally, the library usually has copies or downloadable files of previous exams and students papers that have earned high marks. You can use these to create a template as well.

Most students will use Microsoft Word, as it is the most common program. Word (and most other programs like it) has loads of built-in features that demonstrate the 80/20 principle. The most obvious is the spell check feature. There is no excuse for not using spell check. Papers handed in littered with spelling errors are going to distract the examiner from your content, and your grades will suffer. Another good example of how Word is time efficient is the bibliographic tool. Your references are saved on your computer so you don't have to rewrite them over and over; and when you are finished with your paper, you can simply click a button and your bibliography appears in the style you choose. Simple and easy.

I suggest getting to know Word, play around with the features a bit, learn how to change margins, add page numbers, change spacing and fonts, insert diagrams, make charts, use the bibliographic tool, check spelling and grammar and make a table of content. In the recommended reading at the end of this book, there is a suggestion for a great book that you can use as a quick reference to help you navigate all the different tools available in Word.

The second part of your term paper is the content itself. Once you know how you are expected to present your content (the preferred format), you need to get cracking on putting your brilliant thoughts down on paper. The 80/20 principle can help you here too.

Research is a big part of academic life. It would be strange to hear about submitting a paper without doing some kind of research. Research can be time consuming, but if you form good research habits and know where to look, you can cut down on the amount of time spent doing searches and more time on the content of your paper.

Your speed reading techniques come into play when doing research. You need to quickly skim and preview articles to find out if they are relevant or not. You simply don't have the time to read every possible article that may relate to your topic, so having good preview and skimming skills will help you get through your research pile faster and find the gems that will actually help you. Understanding how to conduct a literature search in your school library is important as it will help you quickly sort through loads of articles. Most schools have online databases and use key-word searches. Be careful to filter your searches for academically reviewed journals if that is important in your field of study.

Another word of caution should be extended to doing "research" on Google or Wikipedia. While both are useful tools in research, be aware that most of what you find on Google will be opinions rather than facts (like reading an "expert's" blog) and that Wikipedia is not peer reviewed with the same academic scrutiny as a scientific journal. This is not to say they are not useful. In fact, Wikipedia often has links to citations that are peer reviewed which you can use within your paper. Be aware these are sources of research you should double check. Also understand that if you are using Google, so are your classmates. An examiner may start to tire of reading the same cited piece of information over and over.

When you have done your research and have begun to write your paper, you may find it helpful to review previous exams, examiner instructions and other students' previous assignments. This helps me to understand what exactly what the examiner was looking for and what they thought deserved a good grade. By understanding what is expected of you, you will be able to ensure that you are focusing your efforts on the parts of your paper which will have the most impact on your grades.

As an example, you may have a lot of business and leadership experience, and decide that on your Organizational Behavior exam you will demonstrate how you have applied different theories during your past work experience. However, the examiner may not be interested in this; they may want you to demonstrate that you know terminology and can discuss different parts of theoretical models in depth. Your real world applications may be valid, but if the examiner isn't interested in them, you can expect a lower score. By reviewing previous exams and examiners notes, you can find out what they were looking for and tailor your answers accordingly.

HOW THE 80/20 PRINCIPLE APPLIES TO TERM PAPERS

The 80/20 principle applies to time input/output and effort input/output when working on your term papers. Understanding what is expected of you will enable you to focus your efforts on producing quality content which is in line with what the examiner expects you to have learnt during the course. Using simple tools in Microsoft Word is a valuable way to maximize your time output when formatting your papers. Make or download a template with all the requirements you need. Doing this once will save you from re-doing it over and over during the next few years. Understanding how to use the features of Word is also important. If you don't know how, ask a friend or get a reference manual. Word also has a "Help" tool you can use, but I personally find it difficult to actually get help with what I need. The book mentioned in the Recommend Reading section was much more useful to me.

Chapter 6

SELF-EDUCATION

I am a firm believer in practical experience. Learning course subjects is valuable and necessary in order to get your degree, but it certainly isn't the end of the road. In fact, after graduation when you find employment, most companies will put you through their own apprenticeship type program to teach you what they think you "really need to know". Taking the time to self-educate yourself is never a waste of time. In fact, you can learn a lot of valuable things outside of a school's curriculum.

A fair comment may be that self-education is time consuming and therefore not in line with the 80/20 principle. I disagree. The issue is not if it is time consuming, the issue is if it is a valuable use of your time resources. By reading, taking courses outside the curriculum or being involved with committees, can you actually enhance your learning and even your marketability when searching for work after graduation? If you weigh the cost/benefits and find these activities to be in your favor, it is then something you should work into your schedule. The main ideas here are to gain new experience/knowledge and to create associations with the knowledge you are learning in your curriculum at school. We will discuss each in turn.

NEW EXPERIENCES/KNOWLEDGE

Involving yourself in activities like committees is a good way to get practical experience. If, for example, you volunteer for a school committee like being the class representative for your subject, you will gain valuable experience in things like leadership, organization and budgeting. The experience you gain from being involved will help by teaching you how to apply the knowledge you are gaining in your classes. It will also look good on your CV and give you practical experience which you can draw upon later in your career. It can also absorb massive amounts of time and, depending on the other people on the committee, can be extremely stressful. Before getting involved, ask yourself the questions that we touched upon in the time management chapter. Will this activity give me good value for my input? Is it a good use of my time, or will it negatively affect my schedule? Each person will be different, but if it is something you find valuable and doable, then go for it.

Enrolling in courses outside the curriculum can also provide great opportunities for self-education. Perhaps you are working on a psychology degree and are interested in developmental psychology. You find a class offered in your community on early childhood education that may be intended for school teachers. You may not get credit towards your degree for taking such a class, but you may find that the opportunity to learn from different viewpoints and the chance to meet and interact with childcare professionals offers you a unique way to build upon the knowledge you are gaining in school. You must decide if this is a useful way to spend your time and economic resources. If you find it is, you should try to absorb as much information as possible.

I can illustrate this point with an example from my own life. I am a certified scuba diving instructor. When I took my teaching certification course, I was offered a few specialty courses that I could add onto my basic course. I thought that since I was using two weeks to get my certification anyway, why not spend an extra week and get a few specializations to go with it. For me, I used the 80/20 principle in my decision making. I asked myself if the time investment was a good one and if the economic investment was worth it. On both cases my answer was yes. I figured that by spending the extra week to get my specialization certifications, I would have to teach about 10 students my new specialization to recover my expenses. I figured, in the courses of a year, I would easily be able to do that. So I enrolled in the extra courses.

Fast forward a few years to when I taught a class of Divemaster students. The Divemaster course is intended to be a first step for those interested in becoming dive professionals. I told my class of students that for an extra fee, I could teach them a specialization in gas mixing. For me this was good business because I already had a captive market audience sitting in front of me who had made the decision to enroll in my Divemaster course. Upselling the specialization course made good sense. However, it wasn't all self-interest on my part. I genuinely thought that this specialization would make my Divemaster candidates better and more employable, so in my eyes it was a win/win situation.

One candidate asked me why they would need such a course. I explained that, as an example, if they were applying to work in a dive shop in Thailand for the summer, and there are two applicants both of whom are Divemasters, but only one is certified to mix enriched air. Since enriched air (Nitrox) is a common request by divers in tropical dive locations, the candidate with the gas mixing certification would be more employable.

The students then had to evaluate if the cost/benefit for them warranted taking the specialization course. Half of my class decided it was because they wanted to actively pursue a career in diving instruction. The others had their own reasons not to take the extra course. The point is that each person used the 80/20 principle (probably without realizing it) to evaluate if this input (financial and time) would provide them with efficient output (new valuable knowledge, better employability, financial gains).

BUILDING ASSOCIATIONS

As we discussed previously, building associations with what you learn in your course work and real world applications is important to retaining knowledge. When we review our notes on a consistent basis we retain the information better. The information is also strengthened when we create associations that we can identify with. Learning about key business concepts like the Invisible Hand, negative externalities and governance may be a bit dry and dull in the confines of a lecture hall, but what if you could learn about it in a more interesting way?

You can, by finding alternative ways to self-educate yourself. In the recommended reading section at the end of this book there is a book about economics and pirates. After reading this book I was able to make interesting associations with key concepts I learnt about in my economics classes at school. The examples given in the book were fun and easy to remember. This type of association strengthens the connection you have to the material and gives your brain a stronger reason to store the information. In a way, it is like re-studying your class notes, because you are reminding yourself of key concepts and giving your brain a new way to interpret the information, thus making it more meaningful. You may think to yourself, "Why would I want to read a book about economics for fun?" Well, when you combine it with pirates, it is certainly a lot more interesting!

The key to self-education is to stimulate your mind into more critical thinking. By going outside the curriculum, you get new ideas, viewpoints and interpretations. When you can begin to question what you learn and discuss it more in-depth, you can then be assured that you are making associations with the knowledge that will allow you to understand it better. Like anything else we discuss in this book, we need to evaluate the 80/20 principle here also. By spending the time to read a book that you won't get credit for, decide if are you wasting time or enhancing your knowledge. Again, each person will be different, but if you can obtain a large output from a small input, you should investigate further to see if it is a valuable use of your resources.

HOW THE 80/20 PRINCIPLE APPLIES TO SELF-EDUCATION

The 80/20 principle applies to self-education in two obvious ways. Firstly, from the perspective of our economics: What can we afford to do? What is a good investment against possible returns? Secondly, it terms of our time resources. We only have so much time to go around, so we have to be sure that any activity related to self-education is not going to turn into a Time Bandit and therefore negate any positive output we could have gained from involving ourselves.

When we evaluate our self-education opportunities from these two perspectives, we can get a better idea of which types of activities we will benefit most from. Remember, we don't always need to benefit financially or technically. Sometimes it's enough just to read a book for the sake of reading it or enroll in a cooking class because it is fun.

Here are a few tips for improving yourself with self-education:

1. *Budget for it.* Put aside a little money each month for self-education. When you put it into your budget and automatically set it aside, you will hardly feel like you are missing it from your paycheck and you will quickly save up enough to open the door to some new opportunities. You can use this money to enroll in a class, purchase books or try new activities. Whatever you use if for is up

to you, but add it as a monthly expense to your budget and you will be happily surprised at how quickly it adds up.

2. *Find low cost alternatives.* Many courses and seminars are offered on campus and through local museums, cultural centers and other community centers that are free to attend. Setting up a book ring with other students is a great way to get access to different books (basically, trading books with others). Open learning courses are also a good way to take classes without needing prerequisites.

3. *Step out of your comfort zone.* Try new things, read different subjects and open your horizons a bit. You will be amazed at how many book subjects are related without actually being about the same thing. Trying a new activity will introduce you to new people and ideas.

4. *Have fun.* Not every course or activity you do has to be academic. Try doing something that is just purely for fun. You meet a lot of great people and might enjoy getting away from the books for a while.

Most forms of self-education are worthwhile if you can fit them into your budget and time schedule. Like anything else when applying the 80/20 principle, ask yourself which activities can you get the most output from. It can be output in the form of academic credentials, business contacts, acquired knowledge or for plain old enjoyment. Whatever it is you are looking for, find the activity that gives you the most of it and then figure out how you can get more of that particular activity.

Chapter 7

MOTIVATION

When we discuss a topic like motivation it becomes too easy to fall for quick fixes as a way to pursue our goals. In reality, the only way to effectively pursue our goals is with proper motivation. For motivation to be effective and useful it has to be internalized so that the motivation actually comes from within. Having a drill instructor screaming in your face or a parent giving you a guilt trip will not provide sufficient long term motivation to actually accomplish your goals. Motivation from within is the most effective way to achieve our goals. Sure, a drill instructor may help you get motivated, but until his goal aligns with your goal, all the motivational speeches/rants in the world won't have a long-lasting effect.

In order to be able to internalize our motivation, we first need to understand what motivation really is. Motivation is a way for us to satisfy our needs. Some needs are necessary for survival, some are important to lead a fulfilling life and others may be superficial. All of us have needs at different levels and unless we can sufficiently motivate ourselves to satisfy these needs, we quickly find ourselves in trouble.

There are many great theories presented by sociologists, psychologists, philosophers and other behavioral experts that help us to understand human needs and how we go about satisfying them. Maslow's hierarchy of needs is a simple model to demonstrate how needs can be ranked, from the most basic needs at the bottom to self-actualization needs at the top of his hierarchy. Other academics have modified his theory to merge levels together or separate them into further subcategories. I will propose my own model, which is based on many of these theories blended together in a way in which I think helps us to understand how motivation relates to students.

Maslow's theory contends that in order for you to satisfy one level of need, you first have to satisfy the needs on levels beneath it. This makes some sense. If you don't have clean drinking water or food to feed yourself or your family, then trying to satisfy an Esteem Need like earning a degree probably isn't your most pressing issue. So, before moving up the hierarchy of needs you would first need to feed, clothe and shelter yourself before worrying about other needs like education. This seems, and is pretty straight-forward.

However, things can become confusing when we get a little further up the hierarchy. Where does security fit in, what does being safe and secure really mean? Some critics give Maslow a hard time for placing sex in the most basic needs category. As university students I will let you decide where that need fits in on your personal hierarchy!

Below I have created a model from the models of researchers like Maslow, McClelland and Alderfer. I will try to explain the model from a student's perspective rather than trying to include needs of a population ranging from the CEO of a Fortune 500 company to a child in a war-torn country.

4 TYPES OF NEEDS

The first level of needs is the Basic Level. This is a students' need for food, clothing, a place to live and basic level of personal safety. Without these needs satisfied, it would be difficult, if not ridiculous, to try to motivate ourselves to seek the satisfaction of other needs.

The second level of needs is the Comfort Level. This is the level in which we try to bring comfort to our lives. We can find comfort by feeling like we belong to a group, having the love of a partner or family. Safety is also a part of this level in that it goes beyond the basic level of safety. For example, safety in the basic level may be the need to not worry about bands of lawless pirates roaming the streets and murdering citizens. In the Comfort Level these are not as extreme as safety needs; we can feel safety in being afforded our privacy or knowing pathways on campus are well lit in the evenings.

The third level of needs is the Adoration Level. This level is where we seek recognition for our achievements and respect from others. Self-esteem and self-image are important parts of this level.

The fourth level is the Self-Actualization Level. This is where, as the Army slogan says, you should "Be all that you can be". We have shown personal growth and are using our abilities.

Being able to satisfy Self-actualization needs isn't the end of the road for us, however. By the time we reach this level, we are generally finding new needs or goals that we motivate ourselves towards. It is this constant journey that helps us become self-actualized, so in a sense we can never really complete this level.

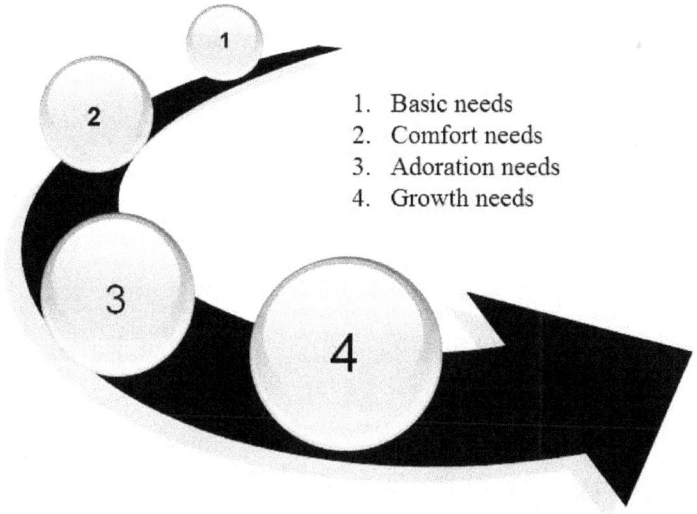

1. Basic needs
2. Comfort needs
3. Adoration needs
4. Growth needs

While it may be necessary to satisfy some lower level needs before trying to move on to others, I don't think that is the case for all of our needs. What motivates us to earn our degree? Is it so we can look after our children (Basic/Comfort Needs) or is it so we get a pat on the back from our father (Adoration Needs)? What is important is how we motivate ourselves to move from level to level.

KEYS TO MOTIVATION

Understanding the keys to motivation ultimately helps us to reach our goals. When we are able to focus our energies on the key elements of motivation, we find ways to utilize the 80/20 principle. Four key elements of motivation are our needs, our attitude, our level of curiosity and our self-discipline. We have covered our needs in the above section, but let's look at the remaining three keys to motivation.

Our Attitude. Having the right attitude is more than just trying to be smiley and cheerful each morning. If we truly want to motivate ourselves it starts with having the right attitude. Your attitude towards somebody or something can quickly help or hinder you from reaching your goals.

When it comes to being a student, I am assuming you are at school (and reading this book, for that matter) because you want to. Something about the idea of going to school motivated you to enroll. Therefore you must have had a certain attitude about school. There are lots of different reasons to enroll in university, but why you enrolled isn't as important as what you do now that you have enrolled. You will need to ensure that your goals and attitude are in line; otherwise you are basically working against yourself.

If your goal is to earn a degree and get a well-paid job, but you begin to find that after a few first-year classes you feel that the subjects are boring and you already know much of the material, your attitude will bring you out of line with your goals. Sure, you may still get your degree, but by changing your attitude you can get more out of your studies.

Being a student in school means you must have two important qualities when it comes to your attitude. The first is to have an open mind. Give your instructors and fellow classmates a chance to make their point. If you are a math expert, but still have to take an introductory math course to complete your requirement, find a way to make it a positive experience. By having an open mind you may find there is something new you can learn, or perhaps you can offer tutorial assistance to others (which creates associations for your brain, strengthening your long term knowledge).

The second point is to have humility. A fond quotation of many instructors is that "there are no stupid questions".

Yes there are, in fact, there are plenty of them and ironically the 80/20 principle works its magic here too (80 percent of stupid questions come from the same 20 percent of students). However, when we act with humility, we stay more positive in our attitude and it is then easier for us to understand that what may be obvious to us isn't obvious to someone else. And at the end of the day, isn't learning why we go to school?

Having humility also helps us to admit that we don't know everything. There is a saying that goes something like, "the more you learn, the more you realize you don't know anything". When we are humble it is much easier for us to see that there are things we can learn in all subjects. If we already knew everything, then what's the point in going to school?

Curiosity. Being curious is a pretty important part of being a student. It is extremely difficult to motivate ourselves to learn something in which we have no interest. That doesn't mean you have to love every subject you take, there will probably be a few that you will be thrilled to be finished with when your exam is over. But, by opening ourselves up a bit and showing curiosity, it is much easier to get into a subject and before long we find that we are actually able to understand and retain the knowledge.

Curiosity also goes hand in hand with self-education, which we discussed earlier. As mentioned earlier, I wasn't curious enough to buy a book solely on economics, but throw in a pirate angle and it became a curious read! Open your horizons a bit and try new things. If you have elective classes that you can spare to take a course outside of your major, then give it a try. There is nothing to lose and you might just find that it was interesting.

Self-discipline. Being self-disciplined is the toughest part of motivation. We've discussed time bandits, procrastination and distractions in previous chapters, but self-discipline is even more important when we discuss motivation. This is because we need to find a way to stay on track. In order to meet our goals, we need to follow steps that take us toward that goal. Along the way there are many distractions, but if we are properly motivated and have a good sense of self-discipline we can stay on track.

The 80/20 principle can really help us with our self-discipline. Whenever we get distracted or lose our momentum, we need to ask ourselves what we really want most. A person with strong self-discipline skills will be able to quickly right their course knowing that the 80 percent of their output will only be obtained by focusing on their goals and looking within for the discipline it takes to minimize distractions.

Self-discipline is not easy and there will be times when you may catch yourself slipping. At these times you need to ask yourself what are the really important things that you want and how can you get them. Being successful in this internal argument will keep you focused on the 80 percent that means the most to you. Once you get the wanted output, you get a sense of accomplishment which makes it easier to motivate yourself the next time you come to a crossroads where your self-discipline is called into question.

Being self-disciplined is also easier when the motivation is your own. When you internalize the motivation for doing something, it is much easier to be motivated to actually carry out the action. As an overly simplified example, a drill instructor can yell at you over and over to do something, but until both of your goals are aligned, you will not have the motivation to do the action.

The drill instructor may scream at you to shine your boots properly, but until you want to have well-polished boots for the sake of having well-polished boots, you won't be properly motivated to have the self-discipline to polish your boots without being yelled at to do it. You may polish your boots out of fear of being yelled at, but the moment the drill instructor is removed from your life, polishing your boots will probably not be important anymore since nobody will get on your case about it. However, if you happen to like having well-polished boots, then the motivation for keeping your boots polished doesn't need to come from a fanatical drill instructor, it comes from within.

GOALS

Now that you are curious about something, humble enough to know you don't know everything and are self-disciplined enough to pursue this knowledge, how do you go about getting it? By setting goals. Goals should tell us how and why we do something. No matter what level of need you are at, there is a reason to get up and do something. If your basic need is to eat, then there has to be a goal for you to achieve and satisfy that need.

The problem with goals is that people don't know how to set them. Being successful in something is extremely motivating, but failing is extremely demotivating. So how can we avoid this problem? By learning how to set proper goals. A proper goal has a clear purpose, a plan and a way to measure it. Too often we make overgeneralized goals that we cannot possibly hope to achieve and therefore fall short, which leads to lower motivation to try again.

Perhaps your goal is to learn French. How will you know when you have learnt French? How will you know when you can stand up and say, "I have been successful in my goal to learn French"? Will it be when you can order soup in a restaurant or when you can have a conversation with a Frenchman without him realizing you are not French?

This is too broad, and therefor the value of the goal is limited. Instead you need to narrow it down and state something that is measureable. By setting a better goal you will be able to identify how you will achieve it and when you have achieved it. Without these factors you are bound to lose your motivation.

When we set a goal, we want it to be something we can actually achieve, and the best way to do this is to make a clear goal. With a clear goal we can begin to outline what it will take to achieve it. After we have clarified our goal we need to be able to say how we will do it. If we want to learn to scuba dive for example, there are steps to go about making that happen. First we need to find out where we can take such a course, then we need to enroll. After that, we need to read the course booklet and attend the lectures. Then we need to do our pool training. Then comes the actual dive training followed by an exam. So far we have a set clear goal and have an outline of what it will take to achieve this goal. Perhaps we can even create sub-goals within the larger goal. For example, set the goal to read chapter two of the scuba manual on Monday.

The next thing we need to do is figure out how we will measure this and know when we have achieved the goal. In the scuba diving example it is easy to know when we have achieved it because, 1. We passed the exam, 2. We performed the skills and dives to the instructor's satisfaction, and 3. We didn't drown.

You get a shiny new certification card that says you are a scuba diver. You've set your goals, identified the steps necessary to achieve your goal and are able to clearly say that you have in fact achieved it.

The point is that without these three components, goal setting can easily become a recipe for disaster. Without clear goals and objectives, there is a greater chance of falling short of your goals and losing the motivation to continue to pursue them.

Goals also need to be realistic. If you want to be rich and think that by smiling and being positive that cash will start to appear in your mailbox, you are only setting yourself up for disappointment. If your goal is to be wealthy, then good for you. Break it down into more manageable and smaller goals. How will you become rich? Start a business? Ok, then that will have many sub-goals as well. Make your goal as specific as possible and it becomes more realistic. It also helps to realize the types of challenges you will face.

Goals need to be attainable. This goes hand in hand with being realistic, but we can take this a little further. If your goal is to become a pilot, but you are blind, this is a fairly unattainable goal. You have to set goals that you can have a chance of achieving. That doesn't mean you shouldn't try things you may fail at, of course you should. You should always challenge yourself, but you also need to know what is attainable. If something is unattainable now, is there a way to work your way up to it with a series of sub-goals?

Goals need to be challenging. If you expect to earn the satisfaction of achieving a goal and the extra motivation that comes with it, your goals need to be challenging. If your biggest goal is to brush your teeth every morning, then you are not really setting the bar too high. Although you achieve your goals, are you sufficiently motivated to try something more challenging next time? By setting a goal that is challenging, there is more to gain by achieving it. The motivation to go for something even better next time will be much stronger when you have mastered a complex challenge.

An equally important part of goal setting is to know what to do when we fall short of our goals. It is unrealistic to expect that we will be successful in everything we do, and in fact it would get a bit boring if we breezed through life without ever falling down once in a while.

When we do fall short of our goals, we can still use this as a motivational tool. What can we learn from our experience? What can we change or do better to attempt to achieve this goal? Is this a goal that we should break down into smaller sub-goals? Is this a goal that is beyond our reach until we do something else first? There are many opportunities to find the silver lining in a failure. Any time we walk away from a setback without evaluating it, it is a lost opportunity for a learning experience.

Reevaluating our experiences, both positive and negative, allows us the opportunity to learn and modify our behavior for the next step in seeking out our goals.

Take every chance you get to try and find out how you can improve. If you feel like you maxed out and this goal was flawless, great! Use those lessons to try to achieve the next goal.

HOW THE 80/20 PRINCIPLE APPLIES TO MOTIVATION

The 80/20 principle is important for motivation because we can use it to help us to set and have the best chance to achieve our goals. When we can identify the activities that we want to do most or that bring us the most satisfaction, we can find ways to do more of them. The 80/20 principle applies to motivation not so much as a time management tool like some of the other points we have made in previous chapters, but more as an instrument for balancing our needs and wants.

When we set goals we can use the 80/20 principle to determine the most efficient way of working towards those goals. The 80/20 principle helps us to eliminate steps that are not useful. We can focus on the steps that will bring us closer to our goals in the most efficient way possible. Even setting the goals themselves can be aided by applying the 80/20 principle. By realizing that a goal is too broad, we can figure out the vital 20 percent of the sub-goals we need to be able to get closer to the ultimate 80 percent reward.

We can also examine what we do in our daily lives that motivates us most to capture the figurative 80 percent of our end goal. If that motivation comes from the people we associate with, the way in which we challenge ourselves or in how we go about completing a task, we can use the 80/20 principle to identify those positive inputs and seek out more of them. When we identify a certain way of motivating ourselves that has led to success, we can try to use the same technique in our other goal setting scenarios. Finding success in achieving a goal is motivating and therefore we should examine what we did right, so we can capitalize on it even more.

Remember that even when we fall short of our goals we can learn useful lessons. Did a particular step or distraction account for a large reason for us not meeting our goal? Is this a small thing that had a big impact? Is this something we can eliminate or change in order to try again? Looking for the inputs that have large outputs (both positive and negative) allows us a valuable opportunity to learn.

By understanding the various levels of our needs, we can use the 80/20 principle to better prioritize what is import for us at the moment. When we understand our need priorities, we can use the 80/20 principle to begin to figure out what are the things we can do that will have the greatest impact on satisfying those needs.

In other chapters, the 80/20 principle helps us to use our time more efficiently. When we discuss motivation, the 80/20 principle helps us to use our energy more efficiently. When we identify the ways to achieve our goals in the most efficient way possible, we become more motivated to push the envelope further. Success brings us the motivation to go higher, go further or to try harder. Identify what works best for you, then duplicated it to achieve better outcomes. When that system doesn't work for a particular task, you can retool it with the help of the 80/20 principle. Asking yourself which elements brought the most success and then finding ways to amplify those elements will build your motivation to continue to work toward your goals.

CHAPTER 8

STUDENT FINANCES

The purpose of this chapter is not to lecture you about how to save money or the dangers of signing up for student credit cards. You will undoubtedly get enough of that from your parents. The purpose rather is to discuss how to live within your means, while still being able to enjoy a student lifestyle and have a little extra cash to do some fun things. The 80/20 principle is all about balance, finding the right balance to help you achieve more. This can also be applied to your finances as a student.

As a student, it is assumed you will be living on a fairly tight budget--unless you are fortunate enough to have somebody bankrolling your next few years. Therefore, it is important to be able to learn how to create a budget and follow it. By creating a realistic budget, we can give ourselves the opportunity to do much more with our money that it looks like at first glance. Even students on scholarship need to know and understand how to control their spending. If you are on a student loan program, a scholarship, being funded by parents or balancing a part time job with your studies, without having a way to control your finances you will quickly find yourself limited in your options.

A popular maxim is "Penny wise, Pound foolish". We will discuss this in more detail below, but essentially what it means is that often we are given tips on how to save a few pennies here and there, while at the same time using most of our Pounds (Dollars, Euros, or whatever) on a few larger expenses. When we focus our time and energy to save pennies but waste the pounds, we are being inefficient with our resources. This is not to say the pennies are not important, they certainly are. However, we also have to look at where the big chunks of our money go. We can use the 80/20 principle to help us identify these costs and begin to learn how to better manage them.

When we create a budget, we should also justify why we spend the money we do. A common example is the cost of a cup of coffee every morning. Over a school year this expense can really add up and there are simple and effective ways to reduce this cost. However, if it is something you can justify in your budget, then you can still have it. Being a student doesn't mean you have to skip nice lattes and only drink instant coffee from a thermos. It just means you have to find a balance within your budget for the things you need and the things you want.

FINDING BALANCE

As any accounting student will tell you, a balance sheet that doesn't add up (or balance) at the end of the month will create problems for a company. We need to think of our own personal budget in the same way. It's a straight forward concept, but one that seems to allude many people when they first start to make their own financial decisions.

Basically, our expenses cannot be more than our income. If we find at the end of the month we are spending more than we are taking in, then we need to make some serious cutbacks to balance our budget. The point of this chapter is not to discuss this principle in depth; rather, we will focus on getting more out of a balanced budget. I will assume that it is obvious that if your expenses exceed your income and you have "luxury" items on the expense side of your budget, you know you need to cut them back or eliminate them.

In order for us to find a good balance we first have to live within our means. This requires keeping our expense less than our income. Once we do this, we can begin to find ways to maximize our income so that we get more output from what we have. Rather than trying to find more income so we can spend more, we will try to find ways to make the income we already have go further.

Of course, having a part time job to supplement your income will give you more opportunities, and probably more expenses. If this is something you can handle in addition to your studies, then you could consider it. However, it is important to realize that you still have to learn and understand how to manage your finances.

THE PENNIES

As mentioned above we often get loads of tips about how to save a few pennies here and there that will add up to "big savings" over the course of a year. While generally speaking these are good ideas, sometimes they can also become counterproductive. A simple example is a man who uses a cell phone app to find the cheapest gas prices in his city. He saves a few cents per liter/gallon but also has to drive 15 minutes out of his way to fuel up. He has used extra time and fuel to buy "cheaper" gas. How much money did he actually save? How much extra time did he spend to save this money? Was it really worth it? Without going deeper into the actual costs and distance driven we don't know for sure, but it illustrates a valid point.

We should evaluate each of our expenses so that we don't end up trying to save a few pennies when it can actually end up costing more (in money, time or energy). I think it is worth keeping in mind that a lot of our expenses are used on service products. Things we could do for ourselves, but pay somebody else for the convenience of having them do it for us. This convenience factor is usually not calculated when discussing how much we can save by making our own coffee rather than buying a cup every day, for example. I think it should be. If you can justify why you pay somebody else to do something you would rather not do yourself, then why shouldn't you enjoy the convenience of it? As long as we don't justify it to the point of causing our budget to become unbalanced, we are safe. Of course, if such an expense creates an unbalance in the budget, we should concede that it is a convenience which we could probably do without.

Here is an example from my personal life. In the dorm I lived in we shared eight washing machines per about one hundred people living in the building. We had to book a time to do our laundry well in advance, risked theft of clothing and the drying machines never really dried our clothes properly. The machines were coin-operating, costing money for each use. I decided this was a huge inconvenience for me. So I purchased a washer/dryer set for our dorm. I asked the others in my dorm if they wanted to chip in, but most didn't want to because spending $75 at once seemed like a bad deal considering they only had to pay $2 per load of laundry in the common room.

So I bought the machine myself for around $500. Now instead of doing laundry once per week and only when I could reserve a time, I could do it whenever I wanted (which was good, because having old gym clothes sitting around for a week is pretty gross). I justified this expense very easily. $2 per load (multiply by two, once for whites and once for colors) per week was going to add up to $208 for the year. I figured I would be in that dorm for two years, and would have spent about $416 on washing in the common room. So I appear to have lost $84 dollars. Well maybe, but the convenience factor of having the wash machine in my dorm meant I could do laundry whenever I wanted, and I ended up doing it more often. If over the two years I did only 21 extra loads of laundry then the expense would have been recouped.

However, here is how it worked out. After a month or two my roommates asked if they could start using the machine rather than walk down to the common room (convenience). I told them they could as long as they chipped in one dollar per wash (just in case the machine needed maintenance, and to cover my original expense). They were happy to because now washing their clothes was cheaper and more convenient. Two of my roommates took me up on the offer and suddenly it was looking like by the middle of the second year the machine would have paid for itself and I may even make a few dollars. In the end I sold the machine to new roommates when I left the building and ended up getting $200 for it.

The point is, by evaluating my expenses and incorporating the convenience factor into the equation, I was able to make a decision that, while appearing to be more expensive, actually saved me money over the long term and was much more convenient. Did putting up $500 mean I had to make other sacrifices to keep my budget from becoming unbalanced? Yes, but with careful budgeting I hardly noticed the few items I had to sacrifice to make it work.

THE POUNDS

The Pounds are our big expenses. The things we spend the largest portion of our income on in any given month. Ordinarily they will include your rent and food (recall the basic needs from chapter 7). Generally speaking, these are the two largest parts of our monthly expenses. You may have other large expenses, but we will focus for a minute on these two as they are common to everyone. We can't avoid needing a place to live or food to eat, so we have to include these in our budgets, but we can identify ways to make these cost items have a smaller impact. Use as an example, looking for a place to rent. Perhaps rent is fairly similar on campus and off, but consider the costs of electricity, internet, washing facilities and public transportation. Can these somehow be minimized by being selective about where you live? If living in one apartment that includes some of these utilities is more expensive than one without, you need to evaluate what the extra costs will actually be. Would you be better off to pay more for rent if it included a fixed price for electricity, television, internet and washing facilities? As an extreme example, some students in Norway actually buy houses for the years that they will attend university. The mortgage is cheaper than renting an apartment when they add in the income from renting out their extra rooms to other students. Of course, it helps to have nice Norwegian parents who are willing to co-sign the mortgage, but it illustrates the same point.

When discussing food expenses there are a lot of ways to cut down on this expense. Not eating properly is not a good way. In actuality, crappy convenience type food generally costs more than good food. Taking the time to make meals which can be frozen and reheated over a few days is a simple way to save money and avoid eating frozen pizza or macaroni and cheese every day. I won't go into detail about how to cut food expenses, as that can easily be found online, but what is important is to think about how to stretch your food budget further rather than increasing or decreasing it. Find creative ways to make your food dollars go further.

MAKING A BUDGET

A budget is only useful if you have the self-discipline to actually follow it. So it is important to make your budget realistic. This may mean making some tough choices about what gets put in and what gets cut out of your budget. Having a realistic budget is important because when you stick to it you are more motivated to continue to follow the budget. When your budget is unrealistic and you fail to meet your goals, the motivation is lost and the entire point of making the budget starts to seem like a waste of time.

Below is a simple example of a budget that you can use. When I was in school, I created my budget using Excel prior to each month. I would sit down and think about what my expenses would be for the coming month. I included my rent, telephone, food, as well as any planned bills and all my extra expenses. When I did this, I had a pretty good idea of what my expenses would be and also how much I would have left over to direct towards other things. I also included extra things like "self-ed", this was a like a mini savings I had each month used to buy new books or attend courses. Sometimes I had to save that line item up for a few months to be able to afford a certain course, but by adding it into my budget it was something I could save for and not use the money on anything else.

The following budget is just an example for the sake of illustrating the point. The amounts are probably not realistic, but you can see how it should look and what types of line items you can include in your budget. Of course, each person will have different expenses depending on their personal priorities and you can add in any that you like.

Date	Income		Expense	Amount
01.08.2008	Student Loan	$1 000		
01.08.2008			Rent	$300
			Groceries	$250
15.08.2008			Telephone	$50
15.08.2008	Parents Support	$150		
01.08.2008			Gym Membership	$75
03.08.2008			Self-Ed	$75
15.08.2008			Savings/Unknowns	$100
26.08.2008			Invoice XYZ	$50
Total		$1 150		$900

As you can see, I have included the income from my student loan and a few dollars that my mom was nice enough to send me. On the expense side I had the usual suspects like rent, groceries and telephone. Then I also added my self-education savings, my gym pass, an invoice I owed and I put aside a little cash for unexpected things that always come up during the month. For example, the previous month I had needed to buy new ink for my printer. You can see that the budget doesn't balance. This is because there needs to be some flexibility. The $250 extra income I seem to have can be used to go out with my friends for a beer or take a date to the movies. Whatever you want to add in you can.

I make two general assumptions with my mini budget. I assume that any money I don't use from the savings/unknown account will be saved separately (I used a cigar box so it wasn't in my account and I wouldn't be tempted to spend it). I also assumed that anything under $20 did not need its own separate line item. If your coffee or smoking habit takes up more that $20 (or whatever limit you set) then include it as a line item in your budget.

This was meant to be a simple budget to help me stay on track with my spending for the month. You can add whatever you want into your budget to suit your needs and make it as specific as you want. The idea here is to give an overview of what you will be spending your money on.

You can modify it throughout the month if other expenses (or incomes) increase or decrease. The usefulness of setting up your budget is to identify your priorities and also to see where you can make cuts if needed. If my budget didn't balance, I would cut out my gym pass, or reduce my self-ed. budget. By being able to see these items in front of me, it made it easier to understand where all my money went.

HOW THE 80/20 PRINCIPLE APPLIES TO STUDENT FINANCES

The 80/20 principle applies to student finances because it gives us the opportunity to identify what expenses are consuming the largest portion of our income. This may not always be the largest expenses. If a certain line item in our budget is responsible for a disproportionate cost, we can evaluate if it is something that needs to be cut back on or eliminated.

By using the 80/20 principle we can find ways to maximize our economy without making unnecessary sacrifices. We can still have some "luxuries" in our budget as long as we plan appropriately and can justify the expense. When we find something that we really need or want in our budget, we can modify other line items to make it work into our budget.

The 80/20 principle also helps us to look past just the dollars and cents. When we include the convenience factor into our analysis, we can decide if not only the economic impact is justifiable, but also the impact on our time and energy. Sometimes paying more is actually better if it serves our purposes more completely. If we have more free time, less stress or more convenience, we can justify why a specific cost should be included in our budget.

The 80/20 principle can even be applied to the bigger picture of financing your education. You can evaluate the risk/reward of taking a student loan or continuing on towards a Master's degree. Could you finance your education by working full- or part-time? Would the extra time it took to get your degree be offset by the money saved in interest by not taking a student loan? The benefit of analyzing these options with the 80/20 principle in mind is that you can include a wider number of variables into your decision making and not just focus on the pennies.

By evaluating where your money will have the most impact, you are using the 80/20 principle to help guide your spending habits. You will need motivation and self-discipline to accomplish your budgetary goals, but by being honest and realistic with your 80/20 analysis you can make your budget go further than you thought it would.

CHAPTER 9

AN 80/20 LIFESTYLE

Leading an 80/20 lifestyle is a vision of our lives the way we would like it to be. It isn't really a goal as we have described in chapter seven, because we can never really reach it. We can however use the 80/20 principle in many parts of our lives to help us take steps towards this overall vision. My description of an 80/20 lifestyle is a life with balance.

In the short and long term there are things we need and want to do. Finding a balance between these things helps us to live a happier and more fulfilling life. When we can identify the important components of the things we need to do, we can accomplish them more efficiently. Likewise, when we understand what it will take to give us more opportunity to include the things we want to do in our lives, we can begin to find ways to make it happen.

As a student you have made a commitment to an academic program, so we can classify this as a "need" to do part of our lives. There are many ways to go about earning a degree, and we can use the 80/20 principle to find ways to make our paths a little easier. However, as student, school is just one part of your life. We have other needs and wants. In order to be an effective student you need to find a balance in your life that supports your physical and mental wellbeing.

In this chapter we will discuss the importance of finding balance in your life and using the 80/20 principle to maximize your outputs to ensure balance. However, I won't go into too many specifics because there are many great sources of information available in books and online blogs about how to lead an 80/20 lifestyle. Check the recommended reading section in chapter 11 for some of these titles.

FINDING BALANCE

There are many challenges associated with being a student. For some people, moving away from home for the first time or going back to school after taking some time off can be difficult. We can overcome some of these challenges by identifying how we can use the 80/20 principle to help us find balance in our lives. Finding balance means that we are able to include our wants in our lives, while at the same time satisfying our needs.

Something we can ask ourselves is what seems like a simple question: "When do I truly feel happy?" This could be when you are around a specific person, engaged in a certain activity or even when you are doing nothing at all (just relaxing on the beach perhaps!). When you can identify one of these times that you are really happy, you should ask yourself, how often do I feel this way? Is this something I can get more of?

There are many examples of people turning their passions or hobbies into successful businesses. These types of people have identified something that makes them happy and they found a way to get more of it. They identified a small part of their lives and turned it into a major part. That is the 80/20 principle in a nutshell. When you can identify the 20 percent of activities that bring you the 80 percent of enjoyment, you should begin to seek ways of focusing more of your energy towards that 20 percent.

You can, of course, also flip the coin and ask yourself, "When I am really unhappy?" These are the times when you find yourself engaged in something (or with somebody) that is just really dragging you down. So you need to figure out how to get less of this input. If you are at a job that you hate, then you need to make a change. Maybe you can just quit, or perhaps something is holding you back from taking such a step. The important thing to do is to begin to evaluate the situation so you can figure out ways to reduce the inputs that hare having such a large negative output.

There are many books that offer guidance in just this topic, so I won't get into it too much here, but the idea is to try to find what makes you happy or unhappy and get more or less of it, accordingly. That's what the 80/20 principle is all about. If you are in a situation where you are unhappy most of the time because of something like a job you dislike, then you are unbalanced. This will have ripple effects into other parts of your life. So too, will being in a positive situation; the ripple effects also spill over into all parts of your life. Finding happiness brings the balance in your life that drives your motivation to do more and do it better.

STUDENT NEEDS

As students we have several needs that we must find a balance for in our lives. When we can identify these needs and how they will help us to be happier we can go about finding ways to prioritize them and make them work into our overall schedule. In this way, we can ensure that the things we have to do get done and the things we want to do are not ignored. Two important needs that we have are described below. Both of these are important for us if we expect to be able to find balance in our lives.

Stimulation: No, it's not what you're thinking! But yes, students need to be stimulated. A person with no interests or hobbies is not leading a very stimulating life. As students we are lucky because most campuses have lots of student groups for all types of interests. Everything from athletic groups to volunteer organizations is available to students who are looking for stimulation outside the classroom. By being involved in a hobby, we get a great chance to get away from the books and meet some new people.

Social Interaction: University environments offer many opportunities for social interaction outside the classroom. As mentioned, there are many groups you can participate in to help you meet other people. Cultural or religious groups, academic study groups and career orientation groups are a great way to meet like-minded people. Being social gives us the opportunity to share ideas, make friendships and try new activities. All of these things can open new doors for us. We may even find somebody or something that we really enjoy. Then we can begin to figure out how to get more of that enjoyment into our lives.

HOW THE 80/20 LIFESTYLE APPLIES TO STUDENTS

The 80/20 lifestyle applies to students in the same way it does to anyone else. It helps us prioritize what is important in our lives. It gives us the opportunity to identify the 20 percent of inputs that bring us the 80 percent of outputs. This can be both positive and negative outputs. That's the great thing about the 80/20 principle; it shows us how to balance our lives. If we are unbalanced in our lives, we can use the 80/20 principle to examine the cause.

When we identify the cause of the unbalance we can begin to make efforts to fix the issues so we find harmony in our lives. We can no more walk around in a state of bliss all day while neglecting our obligations, than we can make no effort to change a situation like a hated job. We have an obligation to ourselves to pursue the things that make us most happy and are of the most benefit to us (and those around us). We should take this obligation seriously because when we do, we start to identify the changes we need to make to bring our lives into balance.

As students we can use the 80/20 principle to help us understand that we have other needs outside the classroom that must be addressed. We cannot ignore our academic obligations, but without addressing other needs like social interaction and stimulation, we will begin to notice that our academic outputs will suffer. Finding the right balance between our obligations and our interests will help us achieve more in the long run.

CHAPTER 10

AFTER SCHOOL

It is never too early to start to prepare for what happens after graduation. In fact, the earlier you start to get your affairs in order, the better. Earning your degree is an important step in moving on towards a graduate program or landing a new position to start your career. Once you have graduated, finding work in your field can be a challenge because you are competing against many other qualified candidates.

The 80/20 principle can help here as well. By understanding the qualities and qualifications future employers find valuable, you can begin to create your portfolio in a way that will help you stand out from the crowd. Human Resource departments get flooded with applications for positions and, not surprisingly, only a few are chosen for further investigation. Although the ratio may not be exactly 20 percent of all candidates who applied are interviewed, the 80/20 principle is being used by HR managers to weed out the candidates who don't meet their needs.

Because we understand the 80/20 principle, we can take steps to put ourselves into that 20 percent group and increase the chances of landing an interview for positions we are interested in. Two important ways we can begin this process is to develop a strong CV or résumé and to collect valuable letters of recommendation. We will discuss each in turn.

Curriculum Vitae

Your CV or résumé is generally the first step in selling yourself to potential employers. Most applications will also require a cover letter, which is more specific to the position, whereas your CV is a general summarization of your work history and academic accomplishments. Tips for creating effective CVs, cover letters and résumés can easily be found online, so I won't cover the formats of these here. Instead we will discuss how your CV is a work in progress.

Collecting information that may be required on job applications is easier to do as you go along rather than waiting until you graduate and trying to backtrack information. I suggest creating a folder on your computer where you can store information that may be important to add to your CV or cover letters in the future.

Most applications will require you to provide dates and perhaps even number of hours worked and salary information for past employment and education. A simple Excel spreadsheet can help you keep this in order and updated. Simply add in information as you complete a course, internship or job. Having these dates will come in handy when you have to fill out applications. Update your CV with any information that you think will be relevant to future employers.

I also recommend that you collect and save copies of your course outlines. You can usually find these online at your school's website. Save these, as they are excellent source material for helping to write cover letters. Instead of just saying you took a Basic Finance course, you can take keywords from the course outline to demonstrate some of the key skills you developed in that course.

Your CV is also an example of the 80/20 principle in that employers don't want to hear about every trivial detail of your past jobs, they just want the most vital bits. Similarly with your education, you don't need to list each course you have taken, instead just stating you have a degree in XYZ will tell your employer what they need to know. If you have taken extra courses or outside training that may be relevant, this is vital information and you should include it.

More and more companies are using external recruiting agents who use online application databases. Unfortunately, what is more efficient for the recruiters' (another example of the 80/20 principle being applied) is not always efficient for the applicant. You may need to log onto their system and input all of your relevant data. Some of the larger companies use the same systems and you can import your data from one to the other. If this is not the case, having saved your information in a folder on your computer will make the task of inputting this data into different systems much easier. Often you are also able to attach your CV and cover letter. Although redundant, the reasoning is that CV formats vary widely and by having all applicants fill out a standardized form, it is easier for the HR people to sort through them. Now if only all the recruiting agencies could agree on one system and standardize that, then we would really be flying!

LETTERS OF RECOMMENDATION

The letter of recommendation seems to come and go in popularity with job recruiters. Sometimes they want lots of references and documentation and other times they don't seem to pay it any attention at all. So it is better to have it and not need it, then need it and not have it. As with keeping your CV current, it is a good idea to try to get letters of recommendation right away from employers, schools or volunteer organizations. Trying to track down people from years ago can turn into a nightmare and a waste of time.

I suggest getting a letter of recommendation from any activity that you think may be useful to your applications in the future. Obviously you want these from your job, but also think about times when you have volunteered your services, courses you have excelled in or apprenticeships you have completed. Although you may not use all of these at the same time, different applications may require you to display different sides of yourself.

When asking for a letter of recommendation, try to do it as soon as possible to the completion of whatever it was you did. This way, your input is still fresh on the recommender's mind and they are better able to give you a useable letter. Depending on the person writing the letter, it may be useful to submit a letter you have written yourself which they can review and sign if they agree with your assessment. In your request you can detail why you need the letter of recommendation and then mention that they can write their own letter or, for their convenience, you have included a letter for them to review.

Some people may see this as being pushy, but the fact is, by writing your own letter you can ensure the contents will be valid and they will be specific enough to be useable. Of course you need to be honest in your assessment, but you can include parts of your job description that you feel you did well and things that are relevant to future positions. I have seen many so-called letters of recommendation which were scarcely more than just an acknowledgement of that fact that a person worked at a certain job. You normally cannot go back and ask the person re-write their recommendation if you are not satisfied with it, so if you think the person is too busy, uninterested in putting in the effort or won't provide you with a useable letter, don't be afraid to offer them a prewritten letter—for their convenience of course! Obviously you won't submit the same template letter to more than one employer. Take the time to make the letter specific and relevant to what you accomplished at that particular job or activity.

HOW THE 80/20 PRINCIPLE APPLIES TO LIFE AFTER SCHOOL

The 80/20 principle will apply to your life after school in the same ways it benefitted you during school. You will use your time management, work habit, and financial skills in the same way. The idea is to become more efficient at recognizing and capturing the inputs that give you the best outputs.

One way to save yourself a lot of time and energy after you graduate is to think of your CV and references as works in progress. Update and collect these documents regularly to make the application processes much easier in the future.

Remember, when applying for jobs you are marketing yourself. So the more specific you can be with the information that you will be sharing, the better off you are. Trying to track down dates and old bosses for references years after the fact can consume a lot of time. By staying on top of this as you go, you will save yourself from many headaches.

You should think of yourself as a brand. How are you going to make yourself one of the 20 percent of candidates that gets noticed by employers and recruiters rather than being one of the 80 percent that gets passed over? The first step to this is having a solid CV and good useable references.

Chapter 11

SUMMING UP THE 80/20 STUDENT

Throughout this book we have often discussed the term efficiency. The 80/20 principle helps us to be more efficient in many facets of our lives. It enables us to recognize and capture more of the good outputs that we seek. However, it is worth mentioning that being efficient at something doesn't necessarily mean it is what is in our overall best interest. We can be extremely efficient at a job which we hate doing. Being good at something and being efficient are not always the same thing. As highlighted in chapter nine, we need to find balance in our lives and to strive for the things, people or experiences that bring us to a better overall place.

The beauty of the 80/20 principle is in its' simplicity. We simply need to learn to evaluate the things we do in our lives. Once we have identified the things that are working for or against us, we can begin to seek more or less of these inputs. As mentioned in the introduction chapter, the exact ratio of 20 percent inputs lead to 80 percent outputs is really just a handy way of explaining the phenomenon. The exact ratio is not important. The importance of the principle lies in understanding that often small portions of our actions have the largest consequences in our lives. A lot of what we do every day is simply not contributing to the steps needed to take us towards a more balanced lifestyle.

All too often we get caught up being busy, but never actually getting any further ahead. The 80/20 principle helps us to identify this busy work and begin to address ways to eliminate or at least reduce it from our daily lives. As a student, the demands on our time, finances, energy and social life can be extremely taxing. It can be easy to get caught up in unproductive grooves. When we learn to utilize the 80/20 principle effectively, we can change this pattern and begin to forge our own more productive and balanced paths. Let's take a few minutes and summarize how unlocking the power of the 80/20 principle will make you a better student.

FINANCES

We re-examine this topic first because, unfortunately, poor control over your economic situation can affect other parts of your life. Anxiety over financial issues can lead to loss of motivation and a feeling of hopelessness that will have negative effects on our lifestyle. However, with some smart planning and realistic financial expectations, we can form a budget that we can meet.

Use the 80/20 principle to examine your expenses. Identifying the costs that are consuming the largest portion of your budget can give you the opportunity to try to find more practical and economical solutions to meeting these requirements in your budget. Being a student generally means that your budget is tight and you have to be aware of where your money goes. The best way to keep control over this is to have a simple budget that you can follow each month.

Setting up your monthly budget gives you the chance to honestly examine where your money is going. Look back at the previous month's budget and see if you were able to meet your obligations or if you have to readjust your budget for the coming month. Did you end up using more money that you thought you would on something that can be reduced or eliminated in the next month? By asking yourself these (sometimes tough) questions, you can begin to shape your budget in a way that you can cover your necessary expenses and still have funds left over to invest in self-education, social functions or even save a little.

As an extra note, it is worth mentioning that most universities have a service to help students find different types of grants, bursaries and scholarships. Don't be discouraged from using these services even if you are not at the top of your class. There are many such awards available for all different types of students. You can find special awards for women, minorities, athletics and even from past employers and other alumni institutions. Take a few minutes to look through the options and you may find something you qualify for. Many of these types of awards will require the type of documentation we discussed in chapter ten, so start that folder on your computer as soon as possible.

MOTIVATION

A true 80/20 student is one who is motivated to work towards their goals and have some fun along the way. Motivation comes from satisfying various needs in our lives. When we are fed and clothed we become motivated to strive for more. When we are safe, we begin to want to push our boarders out a bit and test what's out there in the world.

We can find motivation in our success and our failures if we know where to look. The 80/20 principle helps us to analyze our goals and see what helped or hindered us from reaching them. We are able to identify the people, strategies or steps that made the biggest impact on our ability to accomplish our goals. When we know this valuable information, we can begin to figure out how to get more (or less) of those inputs.

By understand what our needs and wants are we can begin to use our tools such as time management and financial management to figure out ways to go about satisfying these needs and wants. Generally, our needs must be satisfied first, but that doesn't mean our wants are not important. Our wants may be seen as "extras" or "luxuries" but if spoiling yourself with these indulgences works into your schedule and budget then you should go after them. This will lead to more balance in your life, more happiness and ultimately more motivation to continue to work efficiently in ways that will help you continue to enjoy the "wants" in your life while meeting all of your "needs".

TIME MANAGEMENT

Effective time management skills are an essential tool that the 80/20 student needs in their toolbox. When we understand the notion that we cannot truly save time, but only use it more wisely, we are on the right track to understanding the importance of time management. As a student your time resources are spread over many different tasks. Lectures, study groups, self-study, social activities and other tasks that consumer your time can be scheduled so that you can learn to use the time you have in a way that will bring you the most benefit.

The 80/20 principle helps us to recognize when we are using our time in a way that is useful and also when we are becoming the victims of Time Bandits. Time Bandits are those activities, people or tasks that take up a disproportionate amount of time in comparison to the amount of valued output we are getting from them.

By learning to be effective in our scheduling we give ourselves the time we need to complete each task at a high level. We can also ensure that we have adequate time built into our schedules for our "wants" and not just the tasks that we need to do. Having a good schedule can help us to avoid burnout by keeping us on track. We need to give ourselves enough time, breaks and rest to ensure that we can meet our obligations on time and also that we are delivering quality outputs.

Remember from chapter two that we need to rid ourselves of the feelings of guilt if we say "no" to other peoples' requests that we view as unreasonable demands on our time. When you can (and if you want to) help, then by all means do so, but when the request becomes a Time Bandit for you, don't be afraid to decline.

Time management will require you to incorporate some of the other skills you have learnt throughout this book as well. You will need good study habits to ensure that you are using your scheduled time wisely and you will need motivation and self-discipline to stay on track and minimize distractions.

Use the 80/20 principle to examine how you spend your time. Finding out that you can only spend two hours studying effectively will stop you from scheduling a four hour study session where two of the hours become wasted. The 80/20 principle can be used to help identify the optimal time resources which should dedicate to specific tasks. It also helps ensure there is ample time set aside for free time, socializing and other activities that give us the balance in life that we all need.

Proper scheduling is important for the 80/20 student. However, we don't need to become slaves to schedules where we have every minute of every day accounted for by some activity. This will almost certainly lead to a burnout situation. Use your 80/20 skills to schedule the time you need, but also keep your schedule flexible enough to be able to handle some downtime and times when some tasks naturally take longer than expected.

STUDYING AND SELF-EDUCATION

Learning how to study effectively will help you with all aspects of your student life. You will get better grades, retain more of the information and better use your time resources. The objective of studying is to learn and retain the information from your courses. In order to do this you need to understand how to find the information that is important and how to get the most out of your lectures, · study groups and note taking.

Using the 80/20 principle helps us to be able to find the most useful information. When we understand how our textbooks are arranged we can start to apply the 80/20 principle towards our reading and study habits. Most textbooks are arranged in ways to help maximize the usability of the textbook for the student. Highlighted text, notes from the authors, review questions, case studies and other tools help us to understand what the important elements of the book really are.

Learning how to read properly is also very important to the 80/20 student. As students we are required to read and retain a lot of information. By taking a speed reading course or getting a workbook for speed reading, you will learn how to not only read faster, but also read smarter. I truly believe that buying such a course or workbook is one of the smartest investments a student can make (apart from this book of course!). Speed reading workbooks help you to learn how to mark text effectively, how to find information by skimming, how to better retain vital terms and key words, and of course how to work through your reading pile faster.

Self-education, like a speed reading workbook or this book, is a great way to broaden your knowledge base. You brain needs to make associations in order for material to really stick with you for the long term. If you can find an interesting way of making these associations, then you are even more likely to understand and retain the knowledge. Try to put aside a little money each month for some self-education. Even if it takes you a few months to save up for a special course it will be worth it. Also try to step outside your comfort zone once in a while and try a new activity or read a book about something you had not thought of reading before. You may be surprised to learn that you find something new and interesting.

THE 80/20 STUDENT

Now you have many tools at your disposal to help you become a true 80/20 student. Over the next few years as a student you will sharpen these skills and find ways to make them your own. You will be able to carry these skills and attitudes with you onto your career and personal life.

The purpose of this book was not to be a true self-help style book as I am not a Guru who professes to have all the answers. Rather, my objective in writing this book is to stimulate you to think differently about the world around you and how you interact with it. Open yourself to new ways of doing things and different types of knowledge available to you. It will help you capture more of the 80 percent of the valued outputs that we are all striving for. No matter what the figurative 80 percent is for you, you can have it if you practice the 80/20 principle in your daily life.

Your parents may have told you at one point that there are no short cuts in life, or that the only way to getting ahead is to work hard or to "get your nose to the grindstone". This is not necessarily bad advice, but by reading this book I hope you have also come to the realization that the 80/20 principle isn't about taking short cuts. It's about working smarter instead of working harder. Innovation normally makes our lives easier and better. This does not mean we are taking short cuts, it just means we are using new tools at our disposal to get jobs done better. Imagine if you had to write your next term paper with a typewriter and a bottle of liquid white out for correcting errors. Isn't it working smarter to use a PC and spell check? Of course it is. The 80/20 principle is just about working smarter.

The last chapter of this book is some recommended reading I have assembled for you. It is in no way meant to be a complete list of all the possible books out there that could be of use to you. Instead it is just a short summary of a few books which I have enjoyed and thought would be useful for students as they learn more about the 80/20 principle, on their paths to becoming 80/20 students.

Good luck with your studies, I hope you find ways to capture your 80 percent.

CHAPTER 12

RECOMMENDED READING

Here are a few books I thought may be useful or interesting for students who are interested in become 80/20 students. Some are practical guides, some are about the 80/20 principle in more depth and others are just casual self-education books. I have added some information to make it easy for you to find these books in online bookstores and also a brief description and why I thought it may be useful.

10 Days to Faster Reading by The Princeton Language Institute and Abby Marks Beale. (2001)

ISBN 978-0-446-67667-0

This is a speed reading workbook. Some of the most valuable parts are about how to skim properly, mark text effectively and of course exercises for improving your reading speed. There are exercises in each chapter for charting your progress. I found it handy to use an online stopwatch to time the exercises. You can find a simple one at http://stopwatch.onlineclock.net/.

The 4-Hour Work Week: Escape the 9-5, Live Anywhere and Join the New Rich by Timothy Ferriss. (2008)

ISBN: 978-0091923723

This book has many great examples of the 80/20 principle all around us. In it Timothy Ferris describes how he used the 80/20 principle to rebuild his business and restructure his life so he could pursue his happiness while still making money from his business.

The 80-20 Principle: The Secret of Achieving More with Less by Richard Koch. (2007)

ISBN: 978-1857883992

No book about the 80/20 principle would be complete without acknowledging the impact Richard Koch has made with his books on the subject. Koch has a collection of books dedicated to exploring and living the 80/20 lifestyle.

The Decision Book: Fifty Models for Strategic Thinking by Mikael Krogerus and Roman Tschäppeler. (2011) ISBN: 978-1846683954

I added this book because it is filled with models you can use in your presentations. I adapted the learning retention model in chapter four from one of their models in this book. It isn't necessary to re-invent the wheel, so work smarter by using a book like this with models you can use in your reports.

The Invisible Hook: The Hidden Economics of Pirates by Peter T. Leeson. (2009) ISBN: 978-0-691-13747-6

This book is a great example of how to create associations with the knowledge you are getting from your curriculum. This book is about the economics of pirates. By blending the subject of finance with a fun and interesting topic like pirates, this was a very easy read. It is just an example of how you can find interesting books about subjects that you never thought you would bother to explore outside of the classroom.

The Personal MBA: A World-class Business Education in a Single Volume by Josh Kaufman. (2010)
ISBN: 978-0-670-91951-2
This book is an example of self-education. In fact that is the major topic of the book. How you can use self-education to get a world class education without paying for a Master's program. This book will be of particular interest to business students.

Brand You: Turning Your Unique Talents into a Winning Formula by John Purkiss and David Royston-Lee. (2009)
ISBN: 978-09551164-2-1
This book will help you when you begin your job search. It has a lot of good information about branding and marketing yourself to potential employers. It also discusses the importance of building your network.

Word 2010 for Dummies by Dan Gookin. (2010)
ISBN: 978-0470487723
Having this book beside you as you write your term papers will save you from a lot of headaches. By learning how to

use the tools in programs like Microsoft Word properly, you can spend more time polishing your reports rather than trying to figure out how to format them.

The following are some collections of books that can help you expand your knowledge. These would fall into the self-education category. I have included them here because they have a wide range of covered topics that you can look up. Some of the titles may be just for fun or for personal interest, while others are more practical for learning.

The Dummies series. We have all seen these books at the book store. Their big yellow covers are hard to miss, but the fact is these are usually really informative books. The range of topics is impressive and they are reasonably priced. Just type in the search word you are looking for and you will probably find a Dummies book (for example, Sociology for Dummies, Guitar for Dummies etc.). You can find their titles at www.dummies.com.

The Introducing series. These are graphic guides to all sorts of topics. They are short introductions to specific topics. The point of these books is to hit the main topics.

They are a great way to sample a subject you are not sure about to see if you like it. If you do, you can find a more thorough book on the subject. You can find their titles at www.introducingbooks.com.

A Very Short Introduction Series. These are more detailed than the above mentioned series and without the graphics. While still just an introduction to the topic, they are very good at giving you the general overview, and are another effective way to try out some new subjects. You can find their titles at www.oup.co.uk/general/vsi/.

Lee Davidson

SPREAD THE WORD

I hope you have enjoyed 80/20 @ School and that it has provided you with some new ideas that will help you as you work your way through university.

If you have found this book useful, please share it with your fellow students by helping us promote it via Twitter, Facebook and other social media sources. Your feedback is always welcome and I encourage you to leave a rating/review on sites like www.amazon.com and www.barnesandnoble.com.

This book is available in paperback and in eBook format for your convenience.